THE LAST OF THE
KERRYMAN JOKES

THE LAST OF THE KERRYMAN JOKES

by

Des MacHale

THE MERCIER PRESS
CORK AND DUBLIN

The Mercier Press,
4 Bridge Street, Cork
24 Lower Abbey Street, Dublin

ISBN 0 85342 897 2

Illustrations: A. Alcock

To Dominic —
The Last of our Little Jokes?

Typeset by:
Seton Music Graphics Ltd, Bantry, Co. Cork

Printed by Litho Press Co., Midleton, Co. Cork.

INTRODUCTION

Well, all good things come to an end and this is definitely *The Last of the Kerryman Jokes*.

The astonishing success of my previous books *The Book of Kerryman Jokes*, *The Worst Kerryman Jokes*, *The Official Kerryman Jokebook,* and *The Bumper Book of Kerryman Jokes* shows that these jokes are an Irish art-form and not just insult and abuse as a few shallow people believe. Kerrymen and Kerrywomen have not been offended — they treat the jokes with a smile and a shrug of the shoulders as part of the price they must pay for greatness. I feel proud to see all these books on sale in Killarney, Tralee, Dingle, Killorglin, and even in Listowel, the literary capital of the Kingdom.

However, the joke has gone far enough and now the joke is over. Nothing short of an overdraft will persuade me to write another book of Kerryman Jokes. But the need for humour and jokes continues in a world threatened by war, famine, pollution, unemployment, drugs and violence. What we desperately need is more laughter, because laughter eases pain and is the best and most effective medicine in the world, as well as being the cheapest. If you don't believe me, give a copy of this book to a friend who is ill or in hospital and see for yourself the rapid recovery. And there are no side effects except that the patient will be in stitches!

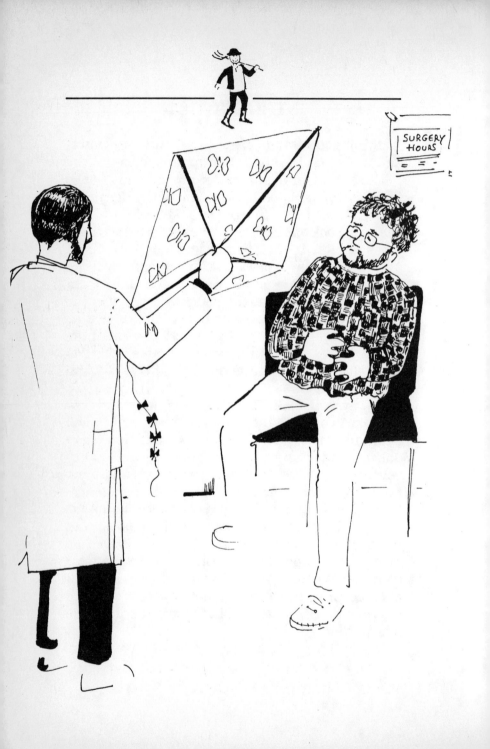

SURGERY
HOURS

A Kerryman was boasting about his son, 'He's one of the cleverest lads in the country,' he told a friend, 'he's always helping the police with their enquiries.'

* * *

Two Kerrymen were taking part in a hairy bacon eating contest in West Cork. The local champion was expected to sweep the boards but he was stopped in his tracks when the first Kerryman said to the other, 'Will we cook it or what?'

* * *

Have you heard about the Kerryman who was caught stealing the lead off the roof of Fort Knox?

* * *

A Kerryman went to his doctor and asked him to give him something for the wind.
The doctor gave him a kite.

This Kerryman went into a posh restaurant with his wife and ordered an expensive bottle of wine.

'Certainly, sir,' said the waiter, 'which year?'

'I'll have it right away,' said the Kerryman, 'if you don't mind!'

* * *

How do you double the value of a Kerryman's car?

Fill the tank with petrol.

* * *

There was this Kerryman who was very self-centred and always wanted to be the focus of attention. If he went to a funeral he would want to be the corpse!

* * *

A Kerryman went into hospital for an operation and woke up shouting, 'Doctor, Doctor, I can't feel my legs!'

'I know,' said the doctor, 'I've just cut your arms off!'

A Kerryman broke into the gambling casino at Las Vegas. When the police caught him he was $3,000 down.

* * *

What do you call a Kerryman in a suit? The defendant!

* * *

A newspaper once published the following retraction of a Kerry news item:
Instead of being jailed for murdering his wife by pushing her downstairs and throwing a lighting oil lamp after her as we reported last week, we believe that the Reverend Roger MacIntosh in fact died unmarried four years ago.

* * *

Have you heard about the Kerry acid bath murderer?
He lost an arm taking the stopper out of the plughole.

11

What do you call a Kerryman in a semi-detached house?
A burglar!

*   *   *

Two Kerrymen were waiting as a bus came along.
'Is this a one-man bus?' the first Kerryman asked the driver.
'It is,' replied the driver.
'We'll wait for the next one,' said the second Kerryman, 'because we both want to get on!'

*   *   *

Why does a Kerryman's car have heated rear windows?
To keep his hands warm while he is pushing it!

*   *   *

Why was the Kerryman jumping up and down on a hedgehog?
He wanted a big chestnut.

13

Have you heard about the Kerryman who burned himself severely at a Halloween party? He was bobbing for chips.

*   *   *

Why do Kerry businessmen not take coffee after lunch?
It keeps them awake all afternoon.

*   *   *

A Kerryman was the oldest man in Ireland and had reached the remarkable age of a hundred and twenty years. A national newspaper sent their top reporter to interview him on the occasion of his birthday.
'To what do you attribute your great age?' the reporter asked him.
'To the fact that it is so long since I was born,' said the Kerryman with a twinkle in his eye.
'Let us be serious,' said the reporter, 'why have you lived to a hundred and twenty?'
'Vitamin pills,' said the Kerryman, 'I've been taking a vitamin pill every day since I was a hundred and ten!'

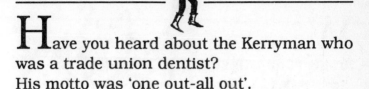

Have you heard about the Kerryman who was a trade union dentist?
His motto was 'one out-all out'.

* * *

First Kerryman: 'The clock goes back this week.'
Second Kerryman: 'You should have kept up with the repayments.'

* * *

Have you heard about the Kerry nightclub that employed a chucker-in?

* * *

This Kerryman went to the doctor and told him that he needed some medical attention.
'What seems to be the problem?' asked the doctor.
'Well doc,' said the Kerryman, 'it's just that I go to the toilet regularly at seven o'clock every morning.'
'That's splendid,' said the doctor, 'why should you be worried about that?'
'I don't get up until eight o'clock,' said the Kerryman.

What does a Kerryman say while making an obscene telephone call?
'Stop telling me the time while I'm talking to you.'

*   *   *

Have you heard about the Kerryman who died in China?
They buried him in a paddy-field!

*   *   *

A Kerryman went to the dentist and asked him to take all his teeth out.
'All of them?' said the dentist.
'Yes,' said the Kerryman, 'all of them.'
So the dentist took out all the Kerryman's teeth.
'April fool,' said the Kerryman, 'all I have is a sore finger.'
Afterwards a friend asked him what it was like having all his teeth out.
'Never again,' said the Kerryman, 'never again.'

Have you heard about the Kerryman who does wonderful work for local hospitals?
He makes people sick.

* * *

A Kerryman applied for a job as head book-keeper with a big firm and was being interviewed by the top directors of the company.
'So you would like to become our head book-keeper, would you?' asked one director.
'That's right,' said the Kerryman, 'I would indeed.'
'And tell me,' said the director, 'what experience have you?'
'A lot of experience,' said the Kerryman, 'I have two library books that are overdue for over six months.'

* * *

Have you heard about the Kerryman who has six O levels?
He had O in mathematics, O in science, O in geography, O in history, O in Latin and O in French.

17

This fellow went into a garage owned by a Kerryman and asked him to check the tyres. The Kerryman walked round the car, kicked each of the tyres in turn and said to him: 'You're fine, you have four of them.'

* * *

A Kerryman went to a psychiatrist and told him he was having some problems.
'Describe your symptoms to me,' said the psychiatrist.
'Sometimes I feel I'm a wigwam,' said the Kerryman, 'and sometimes I feel I'm a teepee.'
'You're too tense,' said the psychiatrist.

* * *

Have you heard about the Kerryman who tunnelled his way to freedom from prison in two months?
He was only serving one month!

* * *

NEWS ITEM: Late last night a Kerryman fell into a upholstery machine. Latest reports say he is now fully recovered.

How do you keep a Kerryman out of your house?
Hide the key under a bar of soap!

*   *   *

A Kerryman was being interviewed for the post of chief accountant and financial officer for a big company and he made a big impression on the board of directors.
'Well,' said the chairman of the board, 'we have decided to appoint you to the position at an annual salary of £38,000.'
'That's great,' said the Kerryman, 'how much a week does that work out at?'

*   *   *

A Kerryman was before the court charged with driving his car at over a hundred miles an hour.
'What is your excuse?' asked the judge.
'Look, your worship,' said the Kerryman, 'I do everything very quickly.'
'Let's see how quickly you can do fourteen days,' said the judge.

Two Kerrymen were drinking late one night and found themselves stranded in town at midnight without even a taxi fare.

'I'll tell you what,' said the first, 'let's break into the bus garage and steal a number 10.'

'Right,' said the second, so after about half-an-hour of the most ferocious banging and crashing he emerged with a number 10 explaining that the number 10s were all at the back.

'Couldn't you have taken a number 14 and we could have got off at the supermarket,' hissed the first Kerryman, 'now I'll go down to the bus stop and you pick me up there.'

But the second Kerryman whizzed past the bus stop and when his friend arrived home an hour later wet and exhausted he explained, 'it was a request stop and you didn't put your hand out.'

*   *   *

A Kerryman went into a hardware shop and asked the assistant if he had long nails (no not the old 'scratch my back' joke).

'Certainly, sir,' said the assistant, 'how long do you want them?'

'I want to keep them,' said the Kerryman.

A Kerryman went to the doctor and told him he was having some digestive trouble.

'What have you been eating?' asked the doctor.

'Snooker balls,' said the Kerryman.

'How many do you eat every day?'

'About a dozen,' said the Kerryman. 'I have three reds for breakfast, a blue and a black for lunch followed by a brown and a blue, four reds for dinner, and a yellow and a pink for tea.'

'That's your trouble,' said the doctor, 'you're not eating any greens.'

*   *   *

This fellow went into a pub and seated at the bar was a Kerryman with the biggest dog he had ever seen.

'Does your dog bite sir?' he asked the Kerryman.

'No,' said the Kerryman, 'my dog is a gentle as a lamb.'

So the fellow went over and patted the dog and the dog nearly bit his arm off.

'I thought you told me your dog didn't bite,' he screamed at the Kerryman.

'That's right,' said the Kerryman, 'but that's not my dog.'

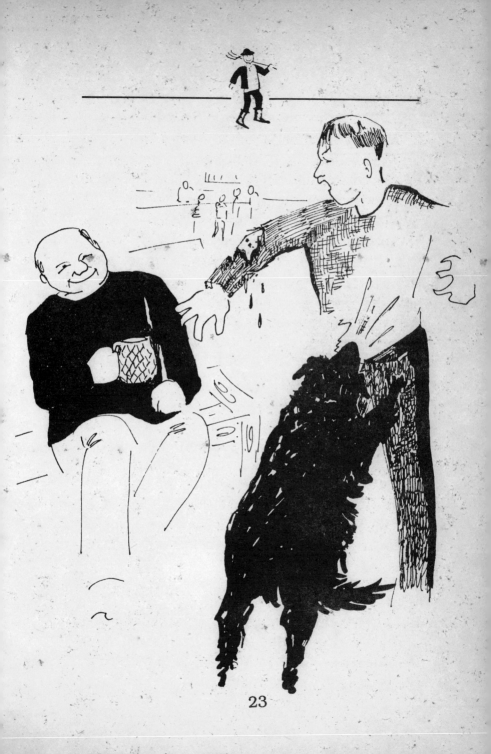

A Kerry plumber was on a world tour and on the second week of the tour he was being shown around North America. The highlight of the visit was a trip of Niagara Falls.

'What do you think of that?' asked the guide, waiting for the amazed reaction.

'If I hadn't left my bag of tools at home,' said the Kerryman, 'I could fix the leak that's causing that.'

A bit taken aback, the guide continued, 'I'll have you know that a billion gallons of water fall over the edge every day.'

'Sure why wouldn't it?' said the Kerryman, 'what's to hinder it?'

* * *

Have you heard about the Kerryman who got a terrific job as a taxi-driver?

He gave it up because he couldn't stand people talking behind his back.

* * *

Have you heard about the Kerryman who wouldn't buy a Japanese transistor radio because he wouldn't be able to understand what they were saying?

A Kerryman rang the police and asked them if they could come and help him.

'What's the trouble sir?' asked the policeman.

'I've locked my keys in the car,' said the Kerryman.

'We'll be round right away, sir,' said the policeman.

'Please hurry,' said the Kerryman, 'it's pouring rain and I've left the sun-roof open.'

* * *

What do you give an eighty year old Kerryman who marries an eighteen year old girl?

Jump leads!

* * *

A Kerryman walked into a clothing store and asked to see the cheapest suit in the shop.

'You're wearing it sir,' said the assistant.

* * *

How do you recognise a posh Kerry household?

They have grapes even when there's nobody sick.

Have you heard about the Kerryman who had to give up his job as a fireman?
It used to take him nearly two hours to slide back up the pole!

*　　*　　*

A Kerryman received an emergency phone call at work that his house had been blown away in a hurricane.
'It couldn't have,' said the Kerryman, 'I have the key right here in my pocket.'

*　　*　　*

A Kerryman was having problems with his weight so his doctor advised him to do some jogging.
'How much should I jog?' the Kerryman asked.
'About ten miles a day,' said the doctor, 'and ring me in a week.' After a week the Kerryman rang to say he was getting on fine with his jogging but that he was seventy miles from home.

Why do Kerrymen wear bowler hats?
To protect their heads from woodpeckers.

* * *

A Kerryman joined the army and was being interviewed by an officer to see what regiment he was suitable for.

'Can you fire a gun?' asked the officer.

'No,' said the Kerryman.

'What can you do?' asked the officer.

'I can take messages, sir,' said the Kerryman.

'Good,' said the officer, 'I think we will assign you to the pigeon corps in charge of vital messages being carried from the front by pigeons.'

The Kerryman underwent a week's intensive training in the pigeon corps and on his first morning on the job a pigeon arrived from the front bearing a message.

'Quick,' said the officer, 'go and see what the message is.'

About an hour later the Kerryman returned, bleeding and torn and covered in feathers and pigeon droppings.

'Well,' said the officer, 'what was the message?'

'Coo, coo,' said the Kerryman.

29

Two Kerrymen were complaining about how lazy their sons were.

'Look at my fellow Seán,' said the first, 'he's so lazy he just sits looking at the television all day.'

'So does my fellow, Mick,' said the second, 'but he's too lazy even to switch it on.'

* * *

An Englishman, an Irishman and a Kerryman were stranded on a little island in the middle of the Pacific Ocean and one day they found a magic bottle. When they rubbed it, a genie appeared and granted them each any one wish they desired.

'I'd like to be back in London,' said the Englishman and he was whisked away.

'I'd like to be back in Dublin,' said the Irishman and he too was whisked away.

'I'm very lonely here all on my own,' said the Kerryman, 'I wish my friends were back again.'

* * *

A Kerryman claimed that Ireland must be the healthiest country in the world.

'Why else,' he asked, 'would the government be closing all the hospitals?'

The general manager of a large banking group was travelling around the country incognito checking up on the efficiency of his branches. He came to a little branch in Kerry where the bank was closed during banking hours and the three clerks were playing poker behind the counter with the bank's money. To give them a fright, he rang the alarm bell three times but none of them moved. However, a few minutes later the barman from the pub across the road brought over three pints of stout.

* * *

A Kerryman got a part in a play where he had only one line to say — 'hark I hear a pistol shot!'
He went around for months beforehand practising his line and driving everybody mad saying: 'hark I hear a pistol shot!'
On the night of the opening performance he came on stage and when the gun went off he shouted: 'what the hell was that noise?'

* * *

Why do Kerrymen carry umbrellas when it's not raining?
Because umbrellas can't walk!

Have you heard about the Kerry seaside village that was reputed to be the dullest place in the world?
One day the tide went out and never came back in.

* * *

First Kerryman: 'I was reading in a book the other day that we use only a third of our brains.'
Second Kerryman: 'What do we do with the other third?'

* * *

Two Kerrymen were out flying when their plane caught fire. The first Kerryman bailed out and pulled the cord of his parachute which opened immediately. The second Kerryman jumped out, pulled the cord, but nothing happened. He went zooming towards the ground at high speed past the first Kerryman. The first Kerryman pulled a knife from his pocket and began to cut at his parachute straps shouting: 'right if you want a race I'll give you one.'

Policeman to the Kerryman: 'What's your name?'
Kerryman: 'Happy Birthday to you, Happy Birthday to you, Happy birthday dear Mick — it's Mick.'

* * *

A Kerryman was before the court charged with riding a bicycle with no light on.
'How do you plead?' the judge asked him.
'Guilty, your honour,' said the Kerryman, 'but insane.'

* * *

How do you recognise a Kerryman's word processor?
The screen is covered in Tippex.

* * *

A Kerryman was asked in an interview if he had ever used a dictaphone.
'No,' he replied, 'I use a telephone like everyone else.'

A Kerryman was taking an intelligence test.

'What is black,' asked the examiner, 'and is worn on the foot in wet weather?'

'I don't know,' said the Kerryman.

'It's a wellington boot,' said the examiner, 'now think before you answer the next question — "what are black and are worn on the feet in wet weather?"'

'I don't know,' said the Kerryman.

'It's a pair of wellington boots,' said the examiner, 'now think before you answer the final question — "who lives in the White House and rules over millions of Americans?"'

'I know that one,' shouted the Kerryman thinking deeply, 'it's three wellington boots.'

* * *

Sign seen on a road in Kerry:
TO MAKE A RIGHT TURN
MAKE THREE LEFT TURNS.

* * *

Have you heard about the twenty stone Kerryman who went on a seafood diet?
He only had to see food and he'd eat it.

34

A Kerry stunt driver decided to go for a world record by driving a bus off a ramp over a line of fifty motorbikes. He very nearly made it but halfway across someone rang the bell.

* * *

This fellow was staying on a Kerryman's farm and he couldn't help noticing that one of the pigs had a wooden leg. Naturally he asked the Kerryman why.

'Well,' said the Kerryman, 'that's quite a remarkable pig. One night when we were all asleep, the house caught fire. That pig roused the entire household and saved two of the children single-handed.

'A few weeks later he was out digging on the land when he discovered oil that's bringing me in a small fortune and recently I've found out that he is working on a new language so that pigs can communicate with human beings.'

'But why the wooden leg?' said the fellow.

'You couldn't eat a pig like that all in one go,' said the Kerryman.

There was this Kerryman in a bar who ordered twenty-seven half-pints of stout and drank them down one after the other. 'Why don't you drink pints instead sir?' asked the barman, 'it would be a lot more convenient.' 'I used to drink pints,' said the Kerryman, 'but the doctor told me they were making me terribly fat, so now I drink half-pints instead.'

* * *

Have you heard about the Kerry surgeon? He had just performed the world's first hernia transplant.

* * *

One Kerryman called round to see another and was astonished to find his friend's son hammering nails into the furniture.
'Why do you let him do that?' he asked.
'It keeps him out of mischief,' was the reply.
'Isn't it a bit expensive?' asked the first Kerryman.
'No,' said the second, 'not a bit — I get the nails free at work.'

Have you heard about the Kerry village that was too small to have a village idiot so they all took turns?

*   *   *

This little fellow parked his car in a narrow little laneway near a Kerryman's house, so the Kerryman came out and asked him to shift it. 'Why should I?' said the fellow, 'after all it's a cul-de-sac, isn't it?'
'Look,' said the Kerryman, 'I don't care what make it is, shift it.'

*   *   *

A Kerryman was out of work so he went around from house to house asking if there were any odd jobs to be done. One fellow felt sorry for him so he gave him a pot of yellow paint and a brush and told him to paint his porch yellow from top to bottom. About an hour later the Kerryman, dripping in paint, came round for his money and said, 'the job is finished, oh, and by the way that's not a Porsche, it's a Mercedes.'

39

A Kerryman went to New York and was driving round in a cab and the cab driver asked him the following riddle — Who has the same father and mother as me but is not my brother and not my sister?

'I don't know,' said the Kerryman.

'It's me,' said the cab driver.

'Begob,' said the Kerryman to himself, 'that's a good one,' so when he got home he tried it out on the lads in the pub.

'Who has the same parents as me but is not my brother and not my sister?' he asked them.

'We don't know,' they all replied.

'It's a cab driver in New York,' shouted the Kerryman.

* * *

How do you recognise a Kerryman's dishwasher?

It's all clogged up with paper plates.

* * *

Have you heard about the Kerry cannibal who went on a self-catering holiday?

He came back with two wooden legs.

How long does it take a Kerryman to write a note to the milkman?
About an hour — even longer if he forgets to write on the paper before he puts it into the bottle.

* * *

A Kerryman went into the post office and asked for a licence for his dog.
'Certainly,' said the clerk, 'what's the name?'
'Fido,' said the Kerryman.

* * *

A Kerryman had his car stolen by a man he thought was his friend and due to a technicality the fellow got off scot free.
'He'll regret it to his dying day,' said the Kerryman, 'if ever he lives that long.'

* * *

How many Kerrymen does it take to make popcorn?
Ten. One to hold the pan and nine to shake the cooker up and down.

43

A Kerryman was travelling by train and the ticket collector asked him where he was getting off.

'Killarney,' said the Kerryman.

'That's impossible,' said the ticket collector, 'we don't stop at Killarney on Tuesdays.'

'Look,' said the Kerryman, 'it's very urgent, I must get off at Killarney today.'

'I cannot break the regulations sir,' said the ticket collector.

'Look,' said the Kerryman, 'it's really very urgent, here's £100, get the driver to slow down a bit and I'll jump off.'

So the ticket collector agreed while warning the Kerryman to keep running after his feet touched the platform or otherwise he would be badly injured.

As the train came into Killarney it slowed to a crawl and the Kerryman jumped off and ran furiously along the platform. As he neared the front of the train a dining carriage attendant grabbed him and pulled him on board saying: 'You're very very lucky to have made it because we don't stop at Killarney on Tuesdays.'

*　　*　　*

Have you heard about the Kerryman who went fly-fishing?
He caught a two pound fly.

* * *

What do you do to a one-armed Kerryman hanging from a tree?
Wave to him.

* * *

What is the happiest five year period of a Kerryman's life?
Junior infants.

* * *

Notice in a newspaper inserted by a Kerryman:
FOR SALE: Twelve Donkeys male and female reasonably priced to clear.
P.S. four of the above have already been sold.

'How is business?' a Kerry trader was asked.

'Terrific,' he replied, 'I bought a tractor for £10,000, traded it for two cars, traded each of them for two motor bikes, traded each of the motorbikes for four racing bicycles and finally sold the racing bicycles for £10,000.'

'But you didn't make a profit.'

'Maybe not,' said the Kerryman, 'but look at all the business I did.'

*　　*　　*

CORKMAN: 'Do you spend all day going up that ladder?'

KERRYMAN: 'No, half the time I come down.'

*　　*　　*

A Kerryman applied for a job as a street cleaner and was told that he would have to take an intelligence test.

'What does psychocybernetics mean?' asked the examiner.

'It means,' said the Kerryman, 'that I'm not going to get the job.'

46

A Kerryman lost an arm but always kept his wristwatch on the stump of the arm he had lost.

'Wouldn't it be more convenient to keep it on the good arm?' a friend asked.

'And what would I wind it with?' said the Kerryman.

* * *

A Kerryman went into a shop and asked for a bottle of sauce.

'Certainly sir,' said the girl behind the counter, 'would you like HP?'

'No,' said the Kerryman, 'I'm paying cash.'

* * *

There's a fantastic new restaurant just opened in Kerry. Inside the door there's a big tank of water. The waiter hands you a net and you can choose any steak you want.

* * *

What is the capital of Kerry?
About £25.

FOREMAN: 'I thought you promised me that you would have that work finished this evening.'

KERRYMAN: 'I'll have it done this evening even if it takes me until tomorrow night.'

* * *

A Kerryman was an undertaker and one day a wealthy young woman came in to his premises and identified a corpse as her father. She gave orders for an expensive and elaborate funeral. Just as she was about to leave, the corpse's lower jaw opened and exposed a set of false teeth.

'My father didn't have false teeth,' she then shrieked, 'cancel that order.' The Kerryman took the body out of the expensive coffin and said to it: 'You fool, you'd have had a first class funeral if only you'd kept your damn mouth shut.'

* * *

What does a golfer get if he asks his Kerry caddie for a sand wedge?

Corn beef in brown bread.

48

Two Kerry businessmen met at Killarney railway station.

'Where are you going?' asked the first.

'Dublin,' said the second.

'You're telling me you're going to Dublin so I'll think you're going to Cork. But I happen to know from another source that you are going to Dublin, so there's no point telling me lies.'

*   *   *

A Kerryman's neighbour called to borrow his donkey but the Kerryman told him it was already lent. Just then the donkey brayed loud and clear in his stable.

'But you said your donkey was already lent,' protested the neighbour.

'He is,' said the Kerryman, 'now who are you going to believe — the donkey or me?'

*   *   *

A Kerryman was called up for jury duty and was asked by the judge if he believed in capital punishment.

'I do,' said the Kerryman, 'if it's not too severe.'

A Kerryman was up before the court charged with having his dog driving his car. 'Do you have anything to say in your defence?' asked the judge.

'Nothing,' said the Kerryman, 'except that I once saw a horse talking on television.'

* * *

A Kerryman went into a pet shop and told the assistant that he wanted a new mirror for his pet budgie.

'Would you like a large one or a small one sir?' asked the assistant.

'I don't rightly know,' said the Kerryman.

'Why not bring him into the shop sir?' said the assistant, 'and we'll try him out in front of a few mirrors and see which one he likes best.'

'That would never do,' said the Kerryman, 'it's for his birthday and I want it to be a surprise.'

* * *

First Kerryman: 'The trouble with Corkmen is that they have no backbone.'

Second Kerryman: 'They have backbone all right if only they would bring it to the front.'

Cork Foreman: 'I can lick any Kerryman working for me.'
Brawny Kerryman: 'You can't lick me and I'm a Kerryman that's working for you.'
Cork Foreman: 'You're fired.'

* * *

First Kerryman: 'What do you think of Dubliners?'
Second Kerryman: 'Between you and me, some of them aren't the full fifty per cent.'

* * *

A Kerryman went to the doctor suffering from some ailment so the doctor prescribed some medicine and told him to take two teaspoonfuls of it every night an hour after taking a bath. A few weeks later the Kerryman returned and told him that there was no improvement in his condition.
'Did you carry out my instructions exactly as I told you?' asked the doctor.
'Not exactly,' said the Kerryman, 'I never managed to drink more than half a bath of water.'

A Kerryman was back home telling his friends in the pub how thousands of people had come to meet him at the airport when he returned to the country.

'I don't believe anyone would turn out to welcome you back to the country,' said the barman.

'There were thousands and thousands of them,' said the Kerryman, 'and if you don't believe me ask Stephen Roche and Sean Kelly, they were on the same flight.'

* * *

A Kerryman was charged with deserting his wife.

'I award your wife £500 a month,' said the judge.

'That's very generous of your honour,' said the Kerryman, 'I'll try and give her a few quid myself as well.'

* * *

Have you heard about the Kerryman who got a job as a public toilet attendant?

They had to let him go because he couldn't remember the prices.

A Kerryman was about to be hung for murder when a telegram arrived. The executioner opened the telegram and began to laugh out loud.

'Have I been given a last minute pardon?' asked the Kerryman anxiously.

'No,' laughed the executioner, 'but you've just won £250,000 in the National Lottery.'

*   *   *

A Kerryman got a job as a zoo keeper to one of the world's rarest female gorillas. The gorilla, however, had refused to mate with all the male gorillas that the zoo authorities had flown in from abroad at great expense. In desperation they asked the Kerryman if he would mate with the gorilla for £5,000. He agreed on three conditions:

(i)   That the gorilla be given a thorough bath.

(ii)   That any offspring resulting from the union be raised as Irish Catholics.

(iii)   That he be given a month to raise the £5,000.

Once there was a serious earthquake in Kerry. It did ten million pounds worth of improvements.

* * *

Kerry preacher at a funeral service: 'My dear brothers and sisters, this corpse was a member of our congregation for the last twenty-five years.'

* * *

A tourist arrived in a Kerry hotel. The porter took his bags and said to him, 'Follow me sir, I'll be right behind you.'

* * *

Two Kerrymen were out driving together.
'Are we getting near a town?' asked the first.
'We must be,' said the second, 'because we seem to be knocking down more people.'
'Well drive slower then,' said the first.
'What do you mean, drive slower?' said the second, 'you're driving aren't you?'

At what Olympic events have Kerrymen won medals?
Heading the shot and catching the javelin.

* * *

Why don't Kerrymen eat Smarties?
It's too much trouble peeling off the shells to get to the chocolate.

* * *

During a flight from Dublin to London a businessman in the non-smoking section of the aircraft suddenly felt the need for a smoke. As there were several vacant seats in the smoking area he asked the hostess if he could change seats. She allowed him to do so and he found himself seated next to a talkative Kerryman.
'It's nice to meet you,' said the Kerryman, 'did you get on just now?'

* * *

Have you heard about the Kerryman who was so tall he had to climb a ladder to shave himself?

57

A Kerryman was suffering from BO so his girlfriend advised him to go home have a bath and afterwards use deodorant and toilet water. Next day she met the Kerryman with his head all covered in bandages.

'What happened?' she asked him.

'The toilet seat hit me on the head,' said the Kerryman.

* * *

Kerryman to garage proprietor:

'Would you have a truncated, hexagonal gasket for a blue van?'

* * *

A court case was in session in Dublin where a German sailor had been charged with being drunk and disorderly.

'I cannot understand a word,' said the judge, 'is there anybody in court who can translate what this man is saying?'

'I'm a fluent speaker of German,' said a Kerryman, 'I'll do it.'

'Good,' said the judge, 'ask him what his name is.'

'Vot iss your name?' said the Kerryman.

Kerryman: 'I think I need a pair of spectacles.'
Man in white coat: 'You certainly do — this is a fish and chip shop.'

* * *

A Kerryman walked into a bar and asked the barman for a pint of less. 'Less?' said the barman, 'I'm not exactly sure if we stock that at the moment. Tell me what exactly is less?' 'I don't know,' said the Kerryman, 'but the doctor told me I would have to drink less from now on.'

* * *

Kerry Preacher: 'Let us all get on our knees and thank God we are still on our feet.'

* * *

What is top of the bestseller list in Kerry this month?
'Memoirs of a Kerry Kamikaze pilot'.

59

A Kerryman bought a fantastic new watch for £5 from a street trader. He was very proud of it because it was guaranteed waterproof, shockproof, anti-magnetic, with 237 jewels and accurate to within one millionth of a microsecond per light year. One night the Kerryman was watching television with his wife when the 'News at Ten' came on the screen. The Kerryman looked at his watch and it said half-past eight. He screamed at his wife, 'have you been messing about with that television set again.'

*　*　*

A conversation between two Kerrywomen:
'How is Mick, your husband?'
'Better, thank God, a lot better.'
'And how is his diarrhoea?'
'Tickenin, thank God, tickenin!'

*　*　*

Have you heard about the Kerryman who won a spot prize at a dance?
He had a total of 4,723 spots.

A Kerryman walked into a bar and ordered nineteen pints of Guinness which he drank one after the other.

'Why do you have to drink so many pints?' a man at the bar asked him.

'See that sign over there?' said the Kerryman, 'it says "nobody served under eighteen."'

* * *

Have you heard about the Kerryman who lost all his teeth?

He slept with his head under the pillow and the fairies took them all during the night.

* * *

Vet: 'Give your cow a tablespoon of this medicine three times a day.'

Kerryman: 'I can't because the cow doesn't use a tablespoon. She drinks from a bucket.'

* * *

Quizmaster: 'Why are cows kept in a pasture?'

Kerryman: 'So they will give pasturised milk.'

61

Have you heard about the Kerry loan shark who lent out half a million pounds?
He immediately skipped town.

* * *

A Kerryman went into a hardware store and asked if he could buy a sink.
'Would you like one with a plug, sir?' asked the assistant.
'Don't tell me they've gone electric,' said the Kerryman.

* * *

Have you heard about the Kerryman who opened a restaurant where people could eat dirt cheap?
It went bust, because people didn't want to eat dirt.

* * *

Lawyer: 'Do you wish to challenge any member of the jury?'
Kerryman: 'I think I could fight that little fellow on the end.'

What happened to the Kerry tadpole?
It turned into a butterfly.

* * *

Have you heard about the Kerryman who failed his driving test?
His car rolled forward on a hill start.

* * *

A Policeman knocked on a Kerryman's door and told him a body had just been washed up on the beach and the authorities thought it might be his.
'What did he look like?' asked the Kerryman.
'Well he was about your height and build,' said the policeman.
'And was he wearing serge trousers?' asked the Kerryman, 'because I always wear serge trousers.'
'Actually he was,' said the policeman.
'What colour?' asked the Kerryman.
'Blue,' said the policeman.
'That couldn't have been me,' said the Kerryman, 'because I always wear black serge trousers.'

A Kerryman asked a Dubliner how he was so smart.

'It's our diet,' said the Dubliner, 'and if you give me £50 I'll sell you some food that will make you smart too.'

'Done,' said the Kerryman, so the Dubliner sold him a pound of Dublin Bay prawns for £50 and the Kerryman ate them. When the Kerryman had bought the third batch of prawns for £50 he said to the Dubliner, 'hold on a minute, I can buy those for £5 a pound in Moore Street.'

'Right,' said the Dubliner, 'just look how smart you're getting already.'

* * *

A rich man hired a Kerrywoman to do his cleaning for him but she failed to give satisfaction. Eventually he had to have a word with her but he tried to put it as gently as possible.

'You know Bridget,' he said to her one day, 'I can write my name on the dust on this desk.'

'Can you now sir?' she replied, 'isn't education a wonderful thing.'

A Kerryman got a job with a big firm.
'Here,' said the boss, 'is a brush. Your first task is to sweep the floor.'
'Hold on,' said the Kerryman, 'I'm a university graduate.'
'OK,' said the boss, 'I'll show you how.'

* * *

Two Kerrymen, a bit the worse for drink, awoke in a room in which the blinds were drawn.
'Is it day or night?' asked the first Kerryman.
'I'll go and have a look,' said the second so he went over to the window, lifted the blind and looked out. Then he walked back and lay on his bed.
'Well,' said the first Kerryman, 'is it day or night?'
'I can't remember,' said the second Kerryman.

* * *

A Kerryman walked into a posh restaurant leaving a trail of mud behind him on the expensive carpet.
'Please clean your shoes before entering our establishment,' said a haughty waiter.
'What shoes?' said the Kerryman.

A Kerryman called into his bank and told the manager that he had just lost his new cheque book.

'Don't worry though,' he assured the manager, 'they won't be of any use to anybody who finds them because I've signed them all.'

* * *

Judge: 'Have you got a competent lawyer to defend you?'

Kerryman: 'No, I haven't, but don't worry about me your honour, because I've got a few good friends on the jury.'

* * *

How do you get rid of a Kerryman's car?
Cover it with rust remover.

* * *

Have you heard about the Kerryman who opened a topless restaurant?
It had no roof.

'What have you got in your pocket?' one Kerryman asked another.

'I'll give you a clue,' said the second, 'it begins with the letter N.'

'A napple,' said the first Kerryman.

'No,' said the second, 'I told you it begins with the letter N.'

'A norange,' said the first Kerryman.

'No, no,' said the second, 'I'm telling you for the last time that it begins with the letter N.'

'Would it be a nonion?' said the first Kerryman.

'You got it at last,' said the second Kerryman.

* * *

What is the definition of a fool?
Someone who drives into a Kerryman's garage and says 'fill her up.'

* * *

First Kerryman: 'What is that on your leg?'
Second Kerryman: 'A birthmark.'
First Kerryman: 'How long have you had it?'

How do you recognise a Kerryman shaving with a electric razor?
He's got the bathroom covered in foam.

* * *

One of the world's richest men had a set of dominoes in which there were huge diamonds instead of spots. One night a Kerryman broke into his house and stole the double blank.

* * *

One Kerryman met another who was carrying two large suitcases.
'Let me tell you about this fantastic new watch I've got,' said the first. 'It's accurate to a millionth of a microsecond and will tell you the time in Tokyo, San Francisco and Melbourne. It's got a built-in calendar, a calculator and a computer. It can tell you the date of any historical event, the time of the tide in any port of the world and the position of the planets at any time in the next thousand years.'
'That's terrific,' said the second Kerryman, 'tell me, what's in the suitcases?'
'That's the battery,' said the first Kerryman.

Have you heard about the new game that is all the rage in Kerry? Two Kerrymen go into a darkened room together and then one of them leaves the room. The other one then tries to guess who left.

* * *

Two Kerrymen went into an employment agency looking for jobs.
'What can you do?' the first was asked.
'I'm a fully qualified pilot,' said the first.
'Good,' he was told, 'we have vacancies for pilots at the moment.'
'How about you?' the second was asked.
'I'm a woodcutter,' said the second, 'one of the best in the business.'
'Sorry,' was the reply, 'we have no vacancies for woodcutters at the moment.'
'But,' said the second, 'how can he pile it if there's no one to cut it first?'

* * *

Corkman: 'Lovely day, isn't it?'
Kerryman: 'I don't know. I'm a stranger here myself.'

71

A Kerryman was asked in an interview what he thought of the American space program.

'I don't know,' he replied, 'I never watch it.'

* * *

How does a Kerryman keep flies out of his kitchen?

He dumps a load of horse manure in his living room.

* * *

KERRY KNOCK-KNOCK.
Knock knock,
Who's there?
Michael Jackson,
Michael Jackson who?
Frank Sinatra.

* * *

The following small ad is said to have appeared in a Kerry newspaper:

FOR SALE: A pair of wellingtons. Worn only once — from 1973 to 1984.

FOR SALE

WORN ONLY ─ ONCE from 1973 - 1984

A Kerryman was asked by a census taker if he had any running water in his house.
'We used to have,' he replied, 'but we had the roof fixed a few years ago.'

* * *

A Kerryman and his wife set up home in an old railway carriage parked in a siding on a closed branch-line. The Kerryman got lots of exercise pushing the carriage up and down the track every time his wife went to the toilet.

* * *

Have you heard about the Kerrywoman who moved from Killarney to Dingle?
She wanted to be nearer her son in America.

* * *

A Kerryman took his best suit in to be dry-cleaned. As he was to collect it he happened to notice that there was a large soup stain on the front. When he pointed this out to the assistant she said to him, 'You can't hold us responsible for that. It was there when you brought it in!'

What do you call a Kerryman driving a Mercedes?
A joy-rider.

* * *

A Kerryman went to the doctor and told him that he got a terrible pain in his arm every time he raised it over his head.
'Don't raise it over your head then,' said the doctor.

* * *

Two Kerrymen were walking along a golf course when suddenly there was a shout of 'fore' and a golf ball came flying through the air and hit one of them on the head.
'Watch out,' said the other Kerryman throwing himself on the grass, 'there are three more to come!'

* * *

What do you call a Kerryman in a detached house?
A squatter.

Two Kerrymen became redundant so they decided to use their redundancy money to set themselves up as painters. The local parish priest asked them to paint the church for him and they offered to do it for £1,000. However, paint proved to be a lot more expensive than they had envisaged and they found their stocks running out before they were even half finished. In desperation they bought gallons of turpentine and added it to their remaining paint and finished the job.

About a month later they called into the church to see how it looked and found large areas of paint peeling from the walls. As they sneaked out of the church they heard a booming voice calling out from above —
'Repaint you thinners.'

* * *

What do you call a Kerryman's open convertible?
A skip.

* * *

Have you heard about the Kerryman who thought that *Ivanhoe* was a Russian gardener?

A Kerryman went to America where he became a policeman. One day he was assigned to keep order at a communist parade. Anxious to do his job well, the Kerryman took his baton and hit an innocent spectator who was just looking at the parade. 'What did you do that for?' said the spectator, 'in fact I'm an anti-communist.'
'Look,' said the Kerryman, 'I don't care what sort of communist you are.'

* * *

A Kerryman took an adult education course in mathematics. He thought the teacher was in love with him because she was always putting kisses on his sums.

* * *

Two Kerrymen became terrorists and were driving around Belfast with a 200 pound bomb looking for a suitable place to plant it. 'Drive a bit more slowly,' said one to the other, 'or this blasted bomb will go off on my knees.'
'Don't worry,' said the driver, 'we've another one in the boot.'

During the visit to this part of the solar system of Halley's comet, a Kerryman was asked what he thought of this heavenly wonder. 'It's a sure sign of frost,' he replied.

* * *

What do you call a Kerryman's car with twin exhausts?
A wheelbarrow.

* * *

A Kerryman complained to a friend at a dance that nobody would dance with him.
'Look,' said the friend, 'to be brutally honest with you, it's the smell from your socks. Go home, change them and when you come back to the dance you'll have girls falling all over you.'
An hour later they met again and the Kerryman complained that there had been no improvement.
'Did you change your socks like I told you?' asked the friend.
'Of course I did,' said the Kerryman, producing the original pair from his pocket.

Have you heard about the Kerryman who had to take a pep-pill every morning to get enough energy to get out of bed so he could go to the chemists to buy his tranquillisers?

* * *

Why did the Kerryman shoot his dog? He wanted a million for killing Rushty.

* * *

A Kerryman got a job on a submarine but got the sack after only a week. He insisted on sleeping with the windows open.

* * *

Quizmaster: 'Who was the first woman in the world?'
Kerryman: 'I don't know.'
Quizmaster: 'I'll give you a clue — she had something to do with an apple.'
Kerryman: 'Would it be Granny Smith?'

A Kerryman went to the optician's and the assistant asked him if his eyes had ever been checked.

'No,' said the Kerryman, 'they've always been blue.'

* * *

A very pious Kerryman was hanging over a cliff by one arm so he prayed for God to save him. A boat passed by in the sea below and the boatman shouted for the Kerryman to jump down and be rescued.

'No,' said the Kerryman, 'God will save me.' A few minutes later a helicopter came dangling its rope ladder over the cliff and the pilot shouted out to the Kerryman to grab the rope and be rescued.

'No,' said the Kerryman, 'God will save me.' Finally a submarine surfaced and the captain called out to the Kerryman to jump. 'No,' said the Kerryman, 'God will save me.'

An hour later he fell off the cliff and was drowned. As he stood before God he said, 'God why didn't you save me?'

'Look,' said God, 'I sent a boat, a helicopter and a submarine, what more could I do?'

81

Optician:'Would you read the letters on this card please?'
Kerryman:'Would you mind reading it to me, because my sight isn't very good?'

* * *

A Kerryman went to the doctor and told him he had just swallowed a bone.
'Are you choking?' the doctor asked him.
'No,' said the Kerryman, 'I'm serious.'

* * *

Have you heard about the Kerryman who stood outside a brothel for two hours waiting for the red light to turn green?

* * *

A Kerryman went to a computer dating agency and he was fixed up with a girl who was a librarian.
On their first date he asked her, 'What part of Libraria are you from?'

A Little Kerry boy was doing his homework so he asked his father where the pyramids were.

'I don't know,' said the Kerryman, 'you should remember where you put things.'

*   *   *

Two Kerrymen were escaping from jail so each of them hid up separate trees. As the police came by with tracker dogs to the first tree one of them shouted out, 'Who's up there?'

'Maiow, maiow,' went the first Kerryman.

'Come away,' said the policeman, 'that's only a cat up there.'

They went to the second tree and the policeman shouted, 'Who's up there?'

'Another cat,' said the second Kerryman.

*   *   *

Have you heard about the Kerryman who tried to commit suicide by taking a hundred aspirins?

After he took two he began to feel better.

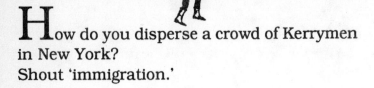

How do you disperse a crowd of Kerrymen in New York?
Shout 'immigration.'

* * *

A Kerryman and his wife were out one evening when burglars broke into their house. They called the police and reported all the things that were missing including jewellery and money.
'Was there any other damage, sir?' asked a policeman.
'No,' said the Kerryman, 'but we had a pot of Irish stew cooking on the stove and one of them did something disgusting in it. We had to throw half of it away.'

* * *

How many Kerrymen does it take to change a lightbulb?
Two.
One says to the other, 'could you switch the light on in here Mick? It's so dark I can't see what I'm doing.'

A Kerryman went to his doctor and told him that he had been feeling so depressed an hour previously that he had taken a hundred of the little yellow sleeping tablets that the doctor had prescribed for him the week before. Now he regretted his decision to commit suicide and asked the doctor to save him. 'Don't worry,' said the doctor, 'those were not sleeping tablets, they were laxatives.'

*   *   *

A Dubliner, a Corkman and a Kerryman each tendered for a big construction job in England, paid for by government money.
'I'll do it for £20,000,' said the Kerryman.
'How is that figure broken down?' asked the boss of the construction company.
'£10,000 for the materials and £10,000 for labour,' said the Kerryman.
'I'll do it for £40,000,' said the Dubliner, 'that's £20,000 for the materials and £20,000 for labour.'
'Look,' said the Corkman, 'my tender is for £60,000. That's £20,000 for you, £20,000 for me and we'll give the other £20,000 to the Kerryman to do the job.'

Three carpenters, an Englishman, an Irishman and a Kerryman were boasting about the high degree of accuracy they used in their work. 'We have to work to the nearest hundredth of an inch,' said the Englishman. 'We have to work to the nearest thousandth of an inch,' said the Irishman.

'That wouldn't do us at all,' smiled the Kerryman, 'we have to get it dead right.'

*   *   *

Have you heard about the Kerryman who thought that Chanel No. 5 was one of those new satellite television stations?

*   *   *

A sophisticated Kerryman was advising his younger brother who was just about to make a trip up the world's longest one way street — the road from Kerry to Dublin.

'Those fellows up in Dublin,' he told him, 'humour them, agree with them. Even if they say that Dublin is bigger than Tralee, agree with them.'

How do you recognise a posh Kerryman?
He picks his nose with his little finger.

*   *   *

What does a Kerry chiropodist have for his breakfast?
Corn flakes.

*   *   *

Have you heard about the Kerryman who was upstairs guarding his money when two other Kerrymen broke in downstairs and watched television?

*   *   *

A Kerryman was working on a building site and one day the foreman told him to go down a deep pit. The Kerryman stepped into the pit and fell thirty feet to the bottom.
'Why didn't you use the ladder?' shouted the foreman.
'I thought that was for coming up,' groaned the Kerryman.

Have you heard about the Kerryman who invented the first telephone?
He had to wait twenty years for someone to invent the second telephone. Then when he rang him up he found it was engaged.

* * *

What were the last words of the Kerry gangster?
Who put that fiddle in my violin case?

* * *

Kerrywoman: 'I keep my goldfish in the bathtub.'
Kerryman: 'What do you do when you want to take a bath?'
Kerrywoman: 'I blindfold it.'

* * *

Doctor: 'You have been very badly injured in an accident. Please tell me your name so I can inform your wife.'
Kerryman: 'There's no need to. My wife already knows my name.'

Then there was the Kerryman who applied for a half-price television licence because he had only one eye.

* * *

Why did the Kerryman cross the road? Because it was the chicken's day off.

* * *

What do you call a Kerryman's boomerang that won't come back?
A stick.

* * *

Have you heard about the Kerryman who crossed a dog with a tortoise?
It goes to the shop and brings back yesterday's newspaper.

* * *

Have you heard about the Kerryman and his wife who were in the steel and iron business?
He did the stealing and she did the ironing.

89

Have you heard about the Kerry electronics expert who has just invented the world's largest microchip?

* * *

Have you heard about the Kerryman who thought that a penal colony was an all-male, nudist camp?

* * *

A Kerryman emigrated to England because he was told that the streets there were paved with gold and that all you had to do was to bend down and pick it up. As he got off the train in London on Saturday night he saw a five pound note lying on the platform so he bent down and picked it up. As he was just about to put it into his pocket he suddenly threw it away saying, 'I won't start until Monday.'

* * *

Have you heard about the Kerryman who was reading a book called *How to Bring up Children*?
One of his kids had just fallen down a well.

A Kerryman and his wife tried to make their sex life more exciting by making love in the bath. They had to give it up because they found the coal too lumpy.

* * *

How does a Kerryman call his dog?
He puts two fingers in his mouth and shouts 'Rover'.

* * *

An old Kerryman was asked if he was in America during the Wall Street Crash.
'Of course I was,' he replied, 'didn't it nearly fall on top of me.'

* * *

What did the Kerryman say when the judge gave him 250 years in prison?
'If I hadn't had a smart lawyer I'd have got life.'

* * *

What do you call a Kerryman's cordless shaver?
A sheet of sandpaper.

This fellow hired a Kerryman to put in concealed lighting in his exclusive new house. The Kerryman papered over all the switches.

*   *   *

Why do Kerrymen's cars have such small steering wheels?
So they can drive with handcuffs on.

*   *   *

A Kerryman was dancing with a girl at a ceili when she asked him if he knew the Walls of Limerick.
'Know them?' said the Kerryman, 'wasn't my sister married to one of them.'

*   *   *

How do you recognise a Kerry shoplifter?
He steals free samples.

*   *   *

What happens to a Kerryman who doesn't pay his garbage bill?
They stop delivering.

Two Kerrymen went to America and the first thing they saw when they landed was a hot dog stand.

'Will you look at that,' said the first, 'they eat dogs in this country.'

'They're very reasonable,' said the second, 'we'll give them a try.'

So they bought two hot dogs and just as they began to eat, one said to the other, 'what part of the dog did you get?'

* * *

Two Kerrymen were working on a building site and one day the first Kerryman's wife arrived to see him while he was climbing up a ladder with half a ton of concrete blocks on his back.

'Don't turn round,' said the first Kerryman, 'but look who's behind you.'

* * *

A Kerryman was complaining to a neighbour about the high cost of food.

'It's not like the old days,' he said to him, 'when you could make a meal out of nothing if you had the stuff.'

A Kerryman was missing for over two weeks so his wife informed the police. One morning the police knocked on her door and told her that her husband's body had been found floating in a canal.

'Yerra that couldn't be him,' she told them, 'because he couldn't swim.'

* * *

A Kerryman was sending his young fellow down to the shop to buy some provisions.

'Get ten kilograms of spuds,' he told him, 'but don't get any big ones because they're too heavy to carry.'

KERRYMEN HIT BACK

What happens if you cross a Dubliner with a boomerang?

You get a dirty smell you can't get rid of.

* * *

What is the difference between a Corkman and a banana?

Some people like bananas.

95

A new young horticultural instructor was appointed to the Kerry region and was doing a tour of the county. He found one old Kerry farmer in the orchard and began to lay down the law about his out-of-date methods of fruit growing.

'Look at this tree,' he said, 'it's not properly pruned, not properly fertilised and it's planted in the wrong place. I'd be surprised if you get ten pounds of apples off that tree.'

'So would I,' said the Kerryman, 'that's a pear tree.'

* * *

What do you get if you walk through Dublin with £50 in your pocket?
Mugged.

* * *

What do you need if you find three Corkmen up to their necks in cement?
More cement.

* * *